Advance Praise

"With these lovely poems Ed Segal pays homage to the wise and courageous mothers of his faith heritage as well as to its ancient desert-dwelling fathers and sons. We hear the soft-spoken yet strong voices of women like Miriam, Hulda, Vashti, Orpah, and Lilith and the fervent, humble prayers and hopeful dreams of contemporary Judaism's leaders and followers. Other poems invite us to remember and mourn those who have been persecuted because of their faith at Auschwitz and elsewhere. Inspired by the quiet wisdom of these poetic voices, we the readers are invited, 'while the tent of peace spreads its wings,' to praise the Near Presence that gave us all human life and form."

> — Dr. Frances Purifoy, Senior Lecturer, University of Louisville Department of Anthropology

Heritage

Edwin S. Segal

Heritage

Edwin S. Segal

Apprentice House
Loyola University Maryland
Baltimore, Maryland

First Edition

Printed in the United States of America

Paperback ISBN: 978-1-62720-141-4
E-book ISBN: 978-1-62720-142-1

Design: Apprentice House Press
Editorial Development: Karl Dehmelt

Published by Apprentice House

Apprentice House Press
Loyola University Maryland
4501 N. Charles Street
Baltimore, MD 21210
410.617.5265 • 410.617.2198 (fax)
www.ApprenticeHouse.com
info@ApprenticeHouse.com

This enterprise began under the influence of the late Karl Kasberg of Harpur College, Binghamton University. It continued with the prodding of Jack Mapanji and Anthony Nazombe, both of Chancellor College, University of Malawi. But the major influence and impetus came from Marcia Texler Segal, who always said it was worth doing.

Contents

Previous Publication Credits

1988

- "Tradition," In *Changing Men,* Summer/Fall

2011

- "Footnotes," in *Poetica Magazine*, Fall, p15
- "Ba'al Tefilah" in *Poetica Magazine*, Spring, p20

2013

- "Memorial" in *Poetica Magazine*,. Summer

2015

- "Witch of Endor," "Deena," "Vashti," "Esther" in *Verse Virtual* August
- "Lilith (in the world)," "Orpah,." Tamar" in *Verse Virtual* September
- "Four Prophets," in *Verse Virtual* October
- "Ancestry," named finalist in Anna Davidson Rosenberg poetry contest, sponsored by Poetica Publishing Company

2016

- Ancestry, *Poetica Magazine*, June

Four Prophets

Prologue

There were only four women,
separate in time and place,
all aware of their mission:
to speak the words in their heads,
facing others with visions
of victory or defeat.
Three are remembered;
one is ignored.

Miriam
(Exodus)

I preserved his life and
gave him his mother's breast,
but he forgot about that.

Heavy of mouth (and brain),
we spoke speeches for him;
then they forgot my part.

I told the words I heard,
which he forgot to write
in the book. He thought them
his own revelations.

I gave them all water;
it always followed me,
and saved them all. When I

died, that they remembered,
because then, it left them.

Devorah
(Judges 4 & 5)

Every day I sat under the tree
settling disputes, casing abrasions.
And then they came, uprooting the trees,
leaving us without harvest or hope

Then I heard the words in my head, and
called to Barak, speaking them to him.
But he was unready, fearing loss.

Sisera was no wolf, and I said
he shall fall to the most defenseless:
a lone woman in her tent, with no
protection but hospitality.

Barak's fears fell before my words, and
Sisera fell to Yael's hammer,
and I sang for us to remember.

Hulda
(II Kings 22:14-20)

Once they thought it strange that I
Would prefer the study house,
debating ideas for
the new world forming around
our cares, and we, hard at it,
began to make that life live.

I was good at it, and they
heard my heart felt passions pour
from mouth and mind, believing
I heard the other world speak.
They called me prophet, but I
preferred scholar, knower of
important things, seer of truth.
I rose in reputation,
So when the king came to me,
I bowed low and told my sight:

The scroll speaks obligation;
We must listen. Holy words
are not to be denied. Read
them to the people, make them
everyone's scripture and law.
And so it came to pass.

Noadiah
(Nehemiah 6:14)

I spoke for the voice of my visions;
physical beauty enhanced my words.
That was when they all came to me,
asking about my dream knowledge.

Who was favored? By whom? Wall builders?
The far away king? How should we go?
I said what was put in my sight
by the call of that other world.

Some heard my words and remembered them,
but not kindly: The great king was far
but not removed; our new walls were
fraught with our worry about him.

Was not the reborn Temple enough,
A place to gather all the people,
to renew our community,
to live at peace with the others?

Epilogue

There were four of us hearing voices
and seeing dreams, when they came to us.
We spoke, as we were charged, when we
were asked for our sight. Our duty
was to speak our visions, confronting
questions put to us by our people.

We had no choice; the other world
commanded us and we complied.
Three of us are remembered and
revered; the fourth is remembered,
but ignored, or branded as false.

Rachel and Leah

(Genesis 29-31)

Together:

> We were sisters, two of six
> matriarchs, bringing two more.
> Different, wed to the same
> man, competing for favor,
> cooperating and yet
> contending, close but apart.

Rachel:

> My skin was bronze from the sun;
> my father worried and when
> Jacob came, he brought labor
> but no trinkets of bright color.
>
> When he moved the stone and watered
> my sheep, I knew I would keep
> his attention and his care.
>
> He saw my needs, and paid heed,
> asking for me to be his.
> Desire ruled; we gave in.

Leah:

> My sight was soft from the sun;
> my father worried and when
> Jacob came, he had no wealth
> and my poor health was unseen.

I was oldest, and so our
father wished me to come first.
His wish ruled and we gave in.

It was a long courtship, so
I gave him his progeny.
Rachel was no match for that.

Together:

We were both well loved, but not
the same; one was fertile and
the other attentive; father
extracted labor for each;
Jacob gave it as asked, but
with a price: herds, future wealth.

Leah:

The magic of spotted goats
and sheep gave us riches; my
children enhanced that gain, so
when the time came to leave,
my children and herds were ready;
his clan was poised for future
greatness. He was blind to it.
We were not and drove him on.

Rachel:

> Leah's seven and Zilpah's
> two were ready to leave, but
> Lavan asked household gods to
> hold us, so I stole them and
> lied to our father, for our
> future freedom, and thereby
> saved our march to Aunt Rivkah,
> ensuring our future fame.

Together:

> Leaving, we met something new:
> swirling, silver storms of sand,
> the chaos of our new life
> come to claim our destiny.
> Jacob knew and sent us to
> one side and he the other.
> And out stepped Esau, but that's
> another story.

Deenah

(Genesis 34)

I am the desert princess,
daughter of Leah, but like
all other desert women,
owned by father and brothers.

Welcomed to the town, meeting
the people of the place, who
were not like S'dom, but made
us kindly welcome for rest,

And the city's prince came out
to meet us and to propose.
No one asked me, but his gilt
face glowed in my heart and mind.

So princess and prince, desert
and city met from the bright
of dawn to the cool of dusk
and from dusk to the new dawn.

Coming together, we were
a wadi in full flood; we
showed our selves to each other
and basked in our shining light.

Again

No one asked me but his guilt
shone in my face. Levi
and Shimon read it right and,
angered on their own behalf.

Their control destroyed, they sought
to dam the wadi's flower,
slaughter and create chaos,
but the desert princess left.

Tamar

(Genesis 38)

I am the oasis palm,
giving life to the sands,
rest to the weary,
succor to the sore,
peace to the fearful.

A sheik of arrogant wealth
gave me to his first son,
for his own sake, but
it was not to be;
that one did not live.

He gave me to his second
son – not for my sake, but
that one would not be
my *Levir*, so he
came to naught and died.

And so Judah was afraid,
blaming me, as men like
to do, when facing
failure, and withheld
his remaining heir.

Now I would not be denied;
there is destiny in
oasis children,
and so he gave me
his fourth, my first son.

I am the life giving palm,
forming future flowers,
creating new clans,
celebrated source
of dynastic lives.

The Witch of Endor

So Saul ....came to the woman at night,
and he said to her, "Please divine for me ...."
I Samuel 28:8

By the time he came to me,
I was living on reputation.
But before him,
I was a see-er growing
in my power, skill and medicine.

Throughout the land
my beauty enhanced my renown
with an aura of bright, magical light
in blazing hair.

My spells and potions gave life
to those in need of my special help,
which came freely
from the spirits who give strength.

But then he came and asked for the shade,
who wanted to rest,
to be done with prophecy.

I warned him against this scheme, but he
would not desist.

The shade came and pronounced doom
and repute for all eternity.
And so it was.

Vashti

(Book of Esther)

I graced his court with beauty and charm,
convincing other wives: take the form
of obedience and work your wills.

His parties turned courtiers into
sycophants, drunk with no power, who
longed to ogle and leer at his household.

Mine were decorous, open to all,
to toasting our freedom from their calls.
Yet, when he called, I would go, as asked.

But I grew tired of the charade, and so,
he was in his cups and called, although
I was drinking with the court women.

He said come!
I said No!

We reveled in my release, but he
heeded his satraps' fear that we
would say the same to all their demands.

As absolute men are wont to do,
he threw me out and sought a new
consort to make him feel powerful.

Well suited to sit on the chair,
She will comfort him, comb his hair
and achieve working her will on him,
while I go my own way.

Esther

(Her own book)

Named for the goddess, but not her, yet.
Miss Persia, known only for beauty.
Serious mistake, but how could they know?

So I came to the king's seat, combing
his beard, stroking ego, asking no boon,
more pleasing than the others, waiting.

And when the time came, I waged war, like
my namesake, using love as a spear,
defeating challengers who wished ill.

When the sun set, they knew who I was;
I strode across the landscape, wreaking
havoc for all who would do us harm.

Gibbets were full and Agag's progeny
filled them all. I had my way
and they learned I am still powerful.

Guarding those who need me, called by my
uncle, I am at their side, always.
And Amalek will never prevail.

Orpah

(The Book of Ruth)

We were sisters, but different
and yet the same.
We walked with her, by her side and
then our world shook.
When it settled, we were alone,
the three of us.
Arid paths lay in front of us,
none desirable.

Naomi said "My road is dry;
I am alone.
Go to your home and start again."
We both said "no."
"Go! Go," she said; "find your new lives.
Be wives again."

Ruth turned and said "only with you."
I turned and said
"I love you too, but go my own way.
Once was enough.
Now, my world takes on its own path."

Lilith

(in our minds)
(a legend)

She's a ghost, a spirit,
our real animation.
As she floats through our space,
we pass through her dream world.

She is mother of demons;
her magic is strong in us;
her children flit through the night
bringing dreams of good and ill.

But we no longer believe,
and demons are mythic mist,
yet still they lope through our days
leaving traces in our nights.

We know her and fear not,
for she is part of us;
fear gives no solution;
we embrace this night demon.

We reclaim her as agent.
Her children are our power,
and we bring her back to
her own world, which is also our's

Lilith

(As she is)

I was his first, but he didn't like my ideas,
too independent for his tastes,
so I went away, to the east.

I sought the demons of the night, found them
and joined their company;
they didn't like my ideas either.

But I joined them anyway and still fared no better.
Feared and shunned by all for millennia,
hemmed in by red ribbons,

protecting the children from my glance,
ineffective amulets
guarding their souls from night dreams.

I waited, and now, in this time:

He still fears me, but she wants a sister
who can bring new ideas to her life,
and so I'm coming back.

The world I fled, my first world, is still my love.

Ancestry

My mythic ancestor, an angry bee,
singer at the site of Moses' triumph,
the Near Presence that gently gave me form,
strides across the lands of my fathers' birth.
Barren hills bloom as she thunders through time
and events, though muted by deaf savants.

Scion of priests, I bend before this shade,
embraced by strength, propelled by history
through ageless ritual cloned from mythic
worlds of divine regulation for life,
to seek the tenth level emanating
from the Source of All, who bore me and is
forgotten in the world beyond my dreams.

My mythic ancestor, clothed in the wind,
the whirlwind's only voice, leaves the dream world
and strides across the deserts of my birth.
And the spirit of the Name Forgotten
passes across the waters of my mind
and chaos crumbles in the birth of light.

Bound

My father was a wandering
Aramean who sought my life.
As well, he was the desert chief
who birthed me with a covenant.

Words carved on parchment echo endless
repetitions, and still I worry
at this paradox without answer,
while time's winds whip through the door of myth.

Born of my mother's ageing laughter,
swaddled in history's purple fringes,
suckled by my father's holy contract,
I am yet bound to my beginnings.

Blue thread binds me to the altar
of my father's faith; an ancient
horn locks my fate to his, and thus
have we wandered alone through time.

And time has grown, while I stand between
generations, bound to first and last.
I am my sire and seek my son's life
with understanding as deep as his.

Ba'al Tefilah

Here I am:
    at the front,
    representative,
    messenger of *cavanah*.

Here I am:
    wrapped in words,
    fringed with weight,
    between two worlds.

Here I am:
    They sent me to speak,
    but I am slow of tongue,
    halt voiced and unsure.

Here I am:
    caught up in custom,
    rapt with ritual,
    in another place.

Here I am:
    bridge from you to us,
    hear the words, I pray,
    of their messenger.

Prayer Leader

Here I am ready to begin;
Words rise, a sweet savour of sound.
My mind's *tallit* covers my head.
Thoughts turn to keeping connections
among us all, through time and space.

We replay history, bridging time,
to our ancestors, who spoke these
words asking peace for their *Ramah*,
as we, for our high places here,
in a world steeped in sacred thoughts.

Tradition

Father and sons stand together
wrapped in tradition's tallis.
For a brief moment the world is
as might have been, fringed with history,
time alive, yet standing still,
while the tent of peace spreads its wings
across their shadow forms bringing
the cool of the morning, when the
Near Presence walks through the garden.
Wings furl: sunrise on reality.
Shadow mist dissolves in present
light; the narrow tent is too small
for living in a world beyond
the scattered wisps of past peace.

A Memory of Auschwitz, 1991

I went to see the place, and now
time and space have been twisted,
and I am still there, as it is
our obligation to be there,
with our mothers and our fathers,
for we must all regard ourselves
as if we too had gone in there
and not come out.

I have been there in that place
where we were herded into the
birch grove, naked, but still human,
and I shall never forget.

I have been there in that place,
in the fire's pit, where we burned,
but kept our humanity,
and I shall never forget.

I have been there in that place
where they tried to kill us,
where they piled the bodies,
and I shall never forget.

I have been there in that place,
in *Amalek's* empty camp;
I have seen my own face there,
and I shall never forget.

Winter Solstice

We sit in the fullness of our season,
Looking at the place where we have been,
And it gapes, a pit of unfilled desire.

The time of filling was not ripe, so we
waited as the world turned to see our needs,
and it did not come, then or even yet.

Indeed, the days are short and do not grow;
the shadow promise is unstuck and flees
the cold light of a dawn that's yet to come.

Raising Money for the Community

Bingo time!
And pull tab fever
burns our sanity.
Big Payoffs outweigh
cautious gains.
Compulsion drops hundreds to win a few.
And we dream on,
losing hard
for a chance to win easy.

Bingo time!
It hurts if we stop,
considering the cost.
Hope springs up; contends
with numbers.
Probabilities reduce our actions.
And we dream on,
in good cause,
for we still have a chance.

Bingo time!
And the hour grows late,
the show is closing
down to final bets
with no hope
for the big diamond or triple seven.
And we dream on
in fever,
for tomorrow is another night.

Yom Kippur

The world didn't stop, but I got off anyway –
for a short time – seeking absolution;
reciting, in chorus, a critical
litany, all part of our communal guilt.

We recite the whole catalogue and I think:
where am I in all this? And then I see
the one line that is mine, boldfaced in my mind;
it stands out, pale in the red glow of others.

I beat my breast, but my sins grow no darker;
the effort is futile, but I am here
for my community, all pale sinners
searching for meaning in this ritual.

When it is over, I feel no better;
my sins still stand; the closed gate brings no relief,
and I choose to live this way every year;
there is no closure.

Kaddish: Remembering

It's the last obligation,
of filial piety,
or sibling competition.
We come to the ancient words,
knowing what most of them mean,
meaning them most of the time.
They are a conversation
with the community, God
and us, beginning a walk
with no finality, for
a lifetime's repetition.
The process has no closure,
starting an endless cycle
of memory and marking.

Memorial

The silent stones stand in serried ranks,
bringing dead order to the chaos of living entropy.
We walk through the rows seeking a place
to stop and remember what had been and will not again.
Stopping at a place helps memory,
keeping it fresh longer than it might have been, and this one
has a stronger claim on being
than most, recalling a life of service to many.
Now we remember, moving forward
to return to the beginning of the endless cycle.

Footnotes

I have aged and have not grown old,
for time is a mobius strip.

Behold:

In all days, at all times,
my desert dwelling fathers march
through the seasons of my mind
while my mothers trail behind,
footnotes to their own history.

In those days, at this time,
Moses' staff gave us dry land, while
Miriam danced to praise God, and
we go on our stiff-necked way,
planting the world to come, sowing
word fields with icons of power.

In those days, at this time,
my brothers waged storied war, while
my mother cooked to praise God, and
we do the same with the light of
mythic candles that last beyond
a week, and for centuries.

In these days, at all times,
my city dwelling sisters march
through the landscapes of my life,
the fifth child, of whom Torah
does not speak, the one ignored.
They do not ask, but shake my
desert world, to make it bloom.

Coming Home

Remember our old history ,
so we can know who we have been,
so we can know where we have been.
But we must beware the snares set
by our thricc told tales, echoing
our millennially misted myths.

We have brought our ghetto walls down
and have ended our long exile.
But we are no longer alone,
and so must learn how to own
only part of our heritage,
ceding the rest to other owners.

We agree on nothing, and so

Writing new history harbors
hidden hooks set to keep us caught
in a mesh that tightens like the
finger traps we build as we have
rebuilt our world – again; the walls
are down, but not yet gone.
The runes are still there to warn us.

If we don't read their hidden rhymes,
the past will still create a maze
showing no way out, surrounded
by how it was, so should be now.
Where is the new path for our hope
that brings security for our dreams?

Border

It's not just a line in the sand,
but a space no one owns,
an idea rattling around
in limbo, argued, creating
division and anxiety.

Borders can be crossed, but on
bridges fraught with customs checks,
exposing our selves to the
gate keeper's critical gaze.

To talk across the space is
to live at the top of our
voices and the edge of our
emotions, losing the
details, where all meaning resides.

And so, we want to be us
and not one of them, mistrusted,
examined without mercy.

Concluded

Naked we come to being, clothing ourselves
with data and their meaning, solving problems
that come our way by happenstance of the world.
Mystery grows; answers are not there and we search
ancestral annals for clues to a reason
for living anomic lives. The plate is set
with things of power, great symbols of those days,
at this time -- all times, all days, all years, all lives.

Each in turn, ritual meaning manifest
before the multitude, gives answer that is
none at all, and so we move on to the next.
Soon it is done; we have completed the course
and sampled the *mana* of the world's icons.
Concluded is the season of our searching.
Concluded is the order of our living.

About the Author

Edwin Segal has been writing poetry since that late fifties, and publishing since 1982. Fortunately, everything earlier than 1974 has been lost. His poems cover a range of topics and styles. Most have a syllabically counted line, irregular slant rhymes and alliteration. Over the course of his writing, he has accumulated a collection of poems concentrating on religion and religious heritage, as well as another focusing on his experiences doing field work in Malawi, where he was awarded a Fulbright Lectureship from 1983-85.

Professor Segal is Emeritus Professor of Anthropology at the University of Louisville. He has done research in Nigeria, Tanzania, Kenya, Malawi, South Africa and Kyrgyzstan. His emphasis has been on gender, ethnicity and national development. He retired from full time teaching in 2006, after forty years, but continues to teach an introductory course, once a year on-line.

Apprentice House is the country's only campus-based, student-staffed book publishing company. Directed by professors and industry professionals, it is a nonprofit activity of the Communication Department at Loyola University Maryland.

Using state-of-the-art technology and an experiential learning model of education, Apprentice House publishes books in untraditional ways. This dual responsibility as publishers and educators creates an unprecedented collaborative environment among faculty and students, while teaching tomorrow's editors, designers, and marketers.

Outside of class, progress on book projects is carried forth by the AH Book Publishing Club, a co-curricular campus organization supported by Loyola University Maryland's Office of Student Activities.

Eclectic and provocative, Apprentice House titles intend to entertain as well as spark dialogue on a variety of topics. Financial contributions to sustain the press's work are welcomed. Contributions are tax deductible to the fullest extent allowed by the IRS.

To learn more about Apprentice House books or to obtain submission guidelines, please visit www.apprenticehouse.com.

Apprentice House
Communication Department
Loyola University Maryland
4501 N. Charles Street
Baltimore, MD 21210
Ph: 410-617-5265 • Fax: 410-617-2198
info@apprenticehouse.com • www.apprenticehouse.com

www.ingramcontent.com/pod-product-compliance
Lightning Source LLC
Chambersburg PA
CBHW072055040426
42447CB00012BB/3132